New Brunswick

New Brunswick

Kumari Campbell

SPEM REDUXIT

Lerner Publications Company

LIBRARY OF CONGRESS
CATALOGING-IN-PUBLICATION DATA

Campbell, Kumari.
    New Brunswick / by Kumari Campbell.
        p. cm. — (Hello Canada)
    Includes index.
    Summary: Introduces the province's geography, history, and people.
    ISBN 0–8225–2764–2 (lib. bdg.)
    1. New Brunswick—Juvenile literature.
    I. Title. II. Series.
    F1042.4.C35 1996
    917.15´1—dc20   95–31043
                                                          CIP
                                                          AC

Manufactured in the United States of America
1 2 3 4 5 6 – JR – 01 00 99 98 97 96

Cover photograph by Jerry Hennen. Background photo by R. Chen/SuperStock.

The glossary on page 68 gives definitions of words shown in **bold type** in the text.

Senior Editor
Gretchen Bratvold
Editor
Colleen Sexton
Photo Researcher
Cindy Hartmon Nelson
Series Designer
Steve Foley
Designer
Julie Cisler

Our thanks to the following people for their help in preparing this book: Peter Larocque, Curator of New Brunswick Cultural History at the New Brunswick Museum, and Vince Warner, a curriculum specialist with the Prince Edward Island Department of Education.

This book is printed on acid-free, recyclable paper.

Contents

Fun Facts

Hartland Bridge

🍁 The longest covered bridge in the world crosses the Saint John River at Hartland, New Brunswick. The bridge stretches 1,283 feet (391 meters), the length of about four football fields.

🍁 Saint John, New Brunswick, became the first official city in Canada in 1785. This makes Saint John Canada's oldest city!

🍁 The world's first chocolate candy bar was made in 1910 at the Ganong Candy Factory in Saint Stephen, New Brunswick.

🍁 One of the world's longest natural sandbars stretches along New Brunswick's northern shore at Chaleur Beach Provincial Park. On one side of the Eel River Sandbar is fresh water, and on the other side is the salty water of the Bay of Chaleur.

At Hopewell Cape in southern New Brunswick, sandstone rocks as tall as five-story buildings rise from the shore of the Bay of Fundy. Because trees grow on top of the rocks, New Brunswickers call them the Flowerpot Rocks. At high tide, the rocks almost disappear beneath the water, leaving only the trees.

Hi! My name is Barkley. As you read *New Brunswick,* I will be helping you make sense of some of the maps and charts that appear in the book.

The Flowerpot Rocks at Hopewell Cape tower above a visitor.

7

The Picture Province

New Brunswick's thick forests, rolling hills, rushing waterfalls, and rocky shores are picture perfect. In fact, these beautiful landscapes have inspired Canadians to call New Brunswick the Picture Province.

Located on Canada's Atlantic coast, New Brunswick is roughly rectangular in shape. The Gulf of St. Lawrence, including the narrow Northumberland Strait, washes against New Brunswick's eastern shore. Across the strait lies the province of Prince Edward Island.

The waters of the Bay of Fundy lap against Grand Manan Island (above) *off New Brunswick's southern coast. A river* (facing page) *winds through the woods of Fundy National Park.*

9

Along New Brunswick's southern shore, a waterfall spills over worn rocks.

A narrow piece of land connects southeastern New Brunswick to Nova Scotia. This strip separates the Northumberland Strait from the Bay of Fundy, which meets New Brunswick's southern coast. The U.S. state of Maine forms the province's western boundary. Chaleur Bay—an inlet of the Gulf of St. Lawrence—and Québec border New Brunswick on the north.

Slightly smaller than the European country of Scotland, New Brunswick is the largest of Canada's three Maritime provinces. The other two Maritimes are Nova Scotia and Prince Edward Island. The Maritimes plus the province of Newfoundland and Labrador to the northeast make up Atlantic Canada. As the westernmost of these Atlantic provinces, New Brunswick is often called the Gateway to Atlantic Canada.

New Brunswick lies in the Appalachians, a stretch of mountains and highlands that reaches into Canada from the United States. Millions of years ago, New Brunswick's land began to fold into ridges. Earthquakes shook the ground and wedged deposits of iron ore, tin, lead, copper, and zinc between layers of rock. Volcanoes spewed hot, liquid rock called lava, which coated the land and cooled into hardened rock.

A hiker in northwestern New Brunswick scans the rounded peaks of the Appalachian region.

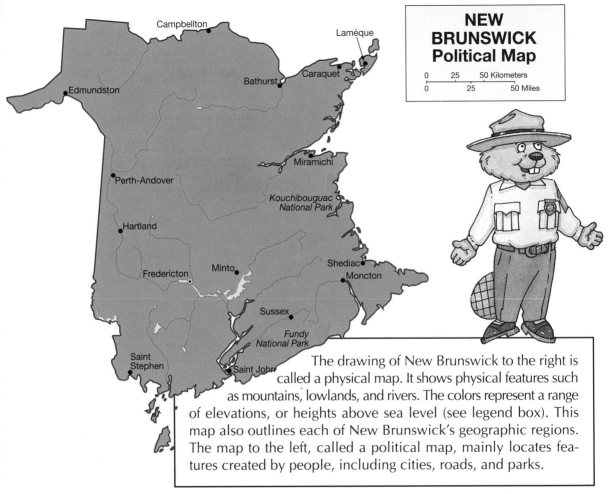

NEW BRUNSWICK Political Map

| 0 | 25 | 50 Kilometers |
| 0 | 25 | 50 Miles |

Campbellton

Laméque

Caraquet

Bathurst

Edmundston

Miramichi

Perth-Andover

Kouchibouguac National Park

Hartland

Fredericton

Minto

Shediac

Moncton

Sussex

Fundy National Park

Saint Stephen

Saint John

The drawing of New Brunswick to the right is called a physical map. It shows physical features such as mountains, lowlands, and rivers. The colors represent a range of elevations, or heights above sea level (see legend box). This map also outlines each of New Brunswick's geographic regions. The map to the left, called a political map, mainly locates features created by people, including cities, roads, and parks.

12

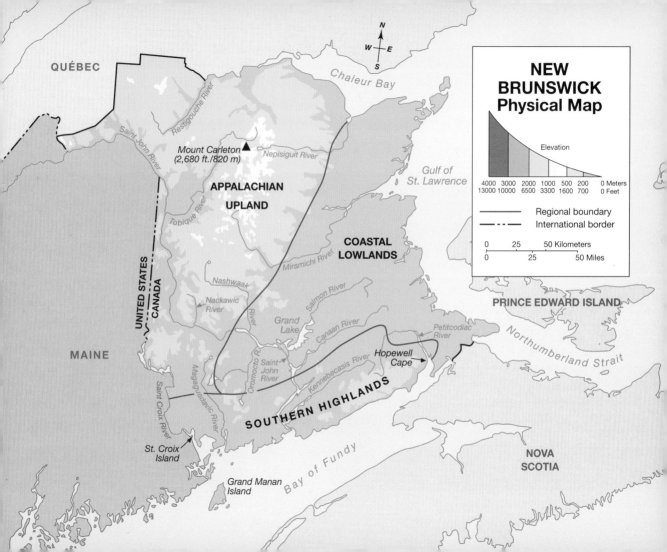

Nowadays New Brunswick is divided into three main regions—the Appalachian Upland, the Coastal Lowlands, and the Southern Highlands.

The rugged mountains of the Appalachian Upland cover the western half of the province. Here Mount Carleton, New Brunswick's highest point,

Black bears (facing page inset) *romp through thick forests in the Appalachian Upland. The Saint John and Tobique Rivers* (right) *meet near Perth-Andover in northwestern New Brunswick.*

rises 2,690 feet (820 m). Thick forests of spruce, fir, pine, maple, and poplar blanket the Upland. These trees provide shelter for moose, black bears, coyotes, and deer.

Beavers, muskrats, and otters swim in the Appalachian Upland's swift rivers. The Saint John, the Restigouche, the Nepisiguit, and the Tobique Rivers have all carved deep valleys through the mountains. In some places, the waterways rush over steep cliffs, creating spectacular waterfalls.

New Brunswick's landscape gradually slopes down to the low plains of the Coastal Lowlands. Farmers grow grain in the wide valleys of the Canaan, the Miramichi, the Nashwaak, and the Salmon Rivers. Miscou Island lies off the region's northeastern shore. Piping plovers nest in the island's white sand dunes.

A boardwalk twists across a bog in Kouchibouguac National Park in eastern New Brunswick.

Palm warblers and other birds live in the lowland's **peat bogs.** Workers harvest the peat—a mixture of decaying plants—which is used in potting soil. Some residents of the Coastal Lowlands also mine the region's deposits of coal and limestone.

Spongy marshes, wind-sculpted sand dunes, and long beaches border the Northumberland shore of the Coastal Lowlands. Workers who live in the region's small fishing villages haul in lobsters and crabs. In summer the warm Northumberland waters draw thousands of swimmers to the region's sandy shores.

Mighty Tides

Tides are the rise and fall, or pulse, of the ocean. This pulse is caused by the force of gravity from the sun and the moon, which pull the water toward them, much like a magnet does. As the ocean rises at high tide, it covers more of the land along a shoreline. At low tide, when the water level goes down, less coastal land is covered.

Most North Atlantic areas have two high tides and two low tides each day. An area experiences high tides when it is closest to the moon and when it is farthest away from the moon. Low tides occur at the midpoints between being closest to and farthest from the moon.

The tides in the Bay of Fundy, off New Brunswick's southern shore, are the highest in the world. The difference between the water level at low tide and at high tide is as much as 56 feet (17 meters)—the height of a five-story building. When the ocean heads into the Bay of Fundy at high tide, some unusual things happen. A wall of water—called a bore—about 2 feet (.6 m) high rushes into the Petitcodiac River at Moncton. And at the mouth of the Saint John River in Saint John, the strong tides force the water to flow up a series of rapids. Called the Reversing Falls, the rapids look like a film being played backward!

High tide

Low tide

Puffins (top) *live on rocky islands in the Bay of Fundy. At low tide, beachcombers and rock collectors walk the wide shore lining the bay* (facing page). *Inland, asters* (bottom) *and other wildflowers brighten fields.*

The rugged Southern Highlands region forms a wide strip of land along the Bay of Fundy. New Brunswick's longest river, the Saint John, flows south past Grand Lake before entering the Bay of Fundy at the city of Saint John. Other rivers in the region include the Petitcodiac, the Kennebecasis, the Saint Croix, and the Oromocto. These rivers weave through roller-coaster hills that slope down to the Bay of Fundy.

In spring and summer, oxeye daisies, black-eyed Susans, purple violets, and other colorful wildflowers bloom in the region's small meadows. But thick stands of trees blanket most of the Southern Highlands. Forests also cover the region's many islands, which dot the Bay of Fundy. Puffins and other seabirds nest on Grand Manan, the province's largest island. Seals and whales splash in the bay's cool waters.

Fog shrouds boats anchored in the Bay of Fundy (left). ***Residents of Fredericton scrape snow and ice from their cars*** (right).

New Brunswick's climate is as varied as its landscape. Inland—especially in the Appalachian Upland—winters are cold and snowfall is heavy. Temperatures dip down to an average of 14° F (–10° C). Inland summers are warm, with readings averaging 67° F (19° C).

Ocean breezes bring milder weather to coastal areas, where winters are warmer and summers are cooler than they are inland. Temperatures average 20° F (–7° C) in winter and 62° F (17° C) in summer. Because of these moderate temperatures, farms along the coast have a growing season that is about 50 days longer than it is in the northwestern mountains.

In the south, the Fundy coast is famous for its fog, which forms when the warm, moist air over the land passes over the cool water of the bay. In winter, snowstorms batter the southern coast. This area gets more snow than anywhere else in New Brunswick.

No matter what the weather is like, Fredericton—New Brunswick's capital—attracts visitors to its historic mansions, theaters, and museums. Sometimes called the City of Stately Elms, Fredericton is known for its tree-lined streets. The city is home to about 45,000 people. Many of these residents work for the provincial government or at the University of New Brunswick, the province's oldest university. Fredericton is located in south-central New Brunswick on the banks of the Saint John River.

New Brunswick's cultural center, the capital city of Fredericton is also known for its stately mansions and tree-lined streets.

Shops and offices (left) *line the sloping streets that lead to Saint John's waterfront. Canada's oldest city, Saint John sprawls along the Bay of Fundy* (below).

About 67 miles (108 kilometers) downstream from Fredericton, at the mouth of the Saint John River, lies the city of Saint John. The province's largest community, Saint John is the industrial hub of New Brunswick. Oil refineries, power facilities, shipbuilding companies, and pulp and paper mills employ many of the city's 77,000 residents. Saint John has one of eastern Canada's key ports. An ice-free harbor allows ships to load and unload at Saint John's docks year-round.

Moncton—New Brunswick's second largest city—sits along the Petitcodiac River in the province's southeastern corner. About 56,000 people live in Moncton, more than one-third of whom speak French as their first language. Moncton earned the nickname Hub City in the late 1800s, when all railway lines to and from the Maritimes passed through this community. The transportation industry is still one of the largest employers in this busy Maritime city.

Native Beginnings

The first people to live in what is now New Brunswick were Paleo-Indians. About 11,000 years ago, these hunters tracked caribou and other large animals through the thick forests of the Maritime region. When game became scarce, Paleo-Indians left the area in search of better hunting grounds.

About 6,000 years ago, Maritime Archaic Indians moved into the region. These early peoples built camps along the coast and speared fish, seals, and walrus for food. In summer the Native people trekked into the forests to gather berries and other plant foods.

The Micmac Indians, who may have descended from Maritime Archaic Indians, settled in the Maritime region about 2,500 years ago. In summer the Micmacs lived along the coast, where they netted salmon and trout and dug up oysters and clams.

The Micmacs hunted with spears and traveled coastal waters in birchbark canoes.

25

In winter the Micmacs moved inland to the shelter of the thick forests. Hunters attracted moose and caribou by blowing into birchbark callers. From birchbark the Micmacs built long canoes and **wigwams** (cone- or dome-shaped dwellings).

The Micmacs shared what is now New Brunswick with the Maliseet Indians, who settled along the Saint John River. Unlike the Micmacs, who often moved their camps, the Maliseets built permanent villages. Here they grew corn, beans, and squash. In the surrounding forest, Maliseet hunters wore beaverskin hoods to disguise themselves as they tracked game. Maliseet traders canoed the rivers to trade with people in other villages.

The Maliseets and the Micmacs were the only groups living in the region when French explorer Jacques Cartier landed at Chaleur Bay in 1534. Cartier claimed all the land that he explored for France. Over time,

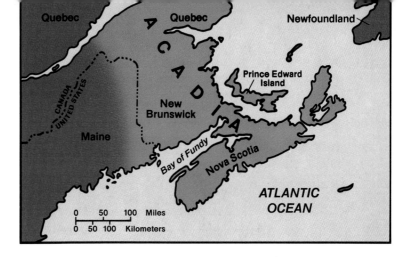

Explorer Jacques Cartier (facing page) *claimed Acadia* (right) *for France. Acadia included all of what is now New Brunswick.*

the French came to call this land L'Acadie, or Acadia. Acadia included almost all of what are now southeastern Canada and part of the U.S. state of Maine.

Soon more Europeans came to Acadia. They fished the fertile coastal waters. The newcomers also established trade with the Native people. The Micmacs and Maliseets gave

Europeans furs in exchange for tools, guns, and other goods. At this time, England wanted to gain control of the valuable fishing and fur industries in Acadia. So to protect its claim to the region, France sent Pierre du Gua de Monts to Acadia in 1603. De Monts and 79 crew members set up camp on Saint Croix Island off the southwestern shore of what is now New Brunswick.

27

Winter on the island that year was harsh. The ocean became icy and too dangerous to sail, cutting the settlers off from the mainland. Many people became ill, and almost half had died by spring. De Monts then moved the settlement across the Bay of Fundy to Port Royal in what is now Nova Scotia. Port Royal became the first permanent French **colony,** or settlement, in the Maritimes.

By the mid-1600s, French farmers had arrived in Port Royal. These newcomers called themselves Acadians and worked hard to build a life in their new homeland. Eventually, Acadian settlements spread westward along the Bay of Fundy into what is now New Brunswick. Farmers planted crops in the fertile but marshy land. They built *aboiteaux,* or **dikes**—long walls that kept the ocean tides from flooding their fields.

Over time, the Acadians came to think of themselves as unique. They were loyal to their families and to their villages instead of to France or to any other country. The Acadians traded both with the French and with the British colonists who lived in New England to the south.

The Micmacs and the Maliseets welcomed the newcomers. They exchanged furs with the Acadians. In return the Native people received guns, metal tools, and clothes—items that helped make their lives easier. Gradually, the Acadians and other Europeans began taking over Native fishing and hunting grounds. Although the Native people fought for their land, the Europeans pushed them northward.

Acadians raised hay and other crops in the fertile soil along the Bay of Fundy.

Meanwhile, Britain and France were battling for Acadia. Throughout the 1600s, the two countries tossed control of the region back and forth. In 1713 France lost almost all of Acadia.

But the French and British could not agree on who owned what is now New Brunswick. To claim this area, the French built Fort Beauséjour on the strip of land between the Bay of Fundy and the Northumberland Strait. The British built Fort Lawrence nearby. In 1755 British soldiers captured Fort Beauséjour, and France gave up the land.

When Fort Beauséjour fell, the British found that about 200 Acadians had defended the French. The Acadians insisted that the French had forced them to fight. But the British

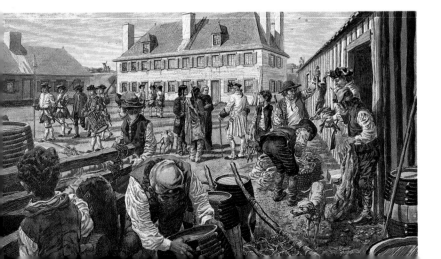

Traders exchange goods at Fort Beauséjour in the early 1750s.

had long thought the Acadians would fight with France if forced to choose sides.

British officials asked all Acadians to sign an oath of loyalty to Britain. When the Acadians refused, soldiers forced them off all British territory. The British set fire to Acadian farms. Families were split up and packed onto separate ships headed for other French colonies. Only a few Acadians managed to escape. They fled to what is now northern New Brunswick, where there were few settlements.

By 1756 the British and French had launched their final battle for control of North America. This conflict was part of the Seven Years' War. Within two years, the British had captured the Fortress of Louisbourg on Cape Breton Island (part of what is now Nova

A British officer announces Britain's plan to remove all Acadians from Acadia.

Scotia). This French outpost had protected all of France's territories in the Maritime region. With the fall of Louisbourg, France lost claim to all land in what is now Maritime Canada.

Acadians and Loyalists

When the Seven Years' War ended in 1763, some Acadians returned. But they found that British settlers from New England had taken over the Acadian farmland. So the Acadians moved north and west. Some built fishing villages along the northern and eastern coasts. Other Acadians farmed the Saint John River valley.

Meanwhile, colonists to the south fought against British rule. By 1776 these colonies had broken ties with Britain and had formed the United States of America. But some residents of the new country were still loyal to Britain and wanted to live in British lands. In 1783, at the end of the American Revolution, more than 60,000 of these people—called **Loyalists**—left the United States. About 15,000 Loyalists settled along the lower part of the Saint John River.

In 1783 thousands of Loyalists from the United States arrived in Parr Town, a small trading post that grew into the city of Saint John.

The Loyalists asked the British king to establish a new colony on the north side of the Bay of Fundy. At this time, the British considered the area a part of Nova Scotia. In 1784 the king divided Nova Scotia and created the colony of New Brunswick, named after the territory of Brunswick-Lüneburg in Germany. In 1785 the Loyalists made Saint John their capital. But because

Nestled in the Saint John River valley, Fredericton became the capital of the colony of New Brunswick in 1785.

A PIONEER PLATEFUL

The early settlers of New Brunswick depended on wild animals and plants for their food. Here are just a few of the dishes that the pioneers cooked up for supper.

New Brunswick Hunters' Stew

Skin, clean, and gut available game (rabbit, squirrel, woodchuck, or bear.) Bring to a boil in a pot of cider. Add herbs, roots, and berries for seasoning. Simmer gently all day.

Moose Nose

Burn one moose snout over an open fire. Scrape clean, then boil until tender. Serve cold, cut in thin slices.

Baked Skunk

Remove musk glands (which would otherwise release a strong odor). Skin and bake until tender. Makes a tasty treat!

the settlement was open to attack by sea, officials moved the capital to the inland town of Fredericton.

As Loyalists settled in the Saint John River valley, the Acadians moved farther north. Although the Acadians and the Loyalists lived in the same colony, their communities were very different. The French-speaking Acadians farmed and fished in the north and east. The Loyalists, who spoke English, mainly lived in the cities of the south.

During the next 50 years, thousands of **immigrants** from the British Isles—mostly from Ireland—poured into New Brunswick in search of work. Many found jobs in the colony's growing logging camps and shipyards. Loggers in the interior cut down tall white pines and floated them down rivers to coastal shipyards. There, builders specialized in crafting small, sturdy cargo ships. Soon Saint John became the busiest shipbuilding center in what is now Canada.

As the colony's lumber and shipbuilding industries boomed, officials in New Brunswick and other nearby British colonies talked of uniting as one country. In 1864 colonial representatives met in Charlottetown, Prince Edward Island. After three years of talks, New Brunswick, Nova Scotia, Ontario, and

Québec formed a new country called the Dominion of Canada. **Confederation**—the official union of the colonies (which became known as provinces)—took place on July 1, 1867.

Workers break up a logjam on the Miramichi River in 1890.

One of the Confederation agreements was to build a railroad that would link the provinces by train. At first the railroad helped New Brunswick earn a lot of money. Fabric,

nails, and other goods made in New Brunswick could be shipped quickly by train and sold in western Canada.

But eventually western manufacturers began producing the same goods and selling them for lower prices. Some of New Brunswick's factories shut down, and many New Brunswickers had trouble making a living.

Iron steamships were invented at about the same time, and people stopped buying the slower, wooden sailing ships made in New Brunswick. Many loggers and shipbuilders in the province lost their jobs. A lot of New Brunswickers left the province to find work in Ontario or in the eastern United States.

New Brunswick's hard times continued throughout the late 1800s and early 1900s. As the economy weakened, the French-speaking Acadians and the province's English-speakers struggled to get along. These two groups still led very different lifestyles. The Acadians continued to live in small, rural towns and fishing villages. They were much poorer than the province's English-speakers. Most English-speakers lived in the cities of Fredericton and Saint John, where jobs were easier to find.

Many Acadians felt that the English-speakers held all the power in the province. The Acadians had only a few representatives in the government, and most laws were made without consulting the Acadian community. But by the 1920s, the Acadians had started their own colleges, which educated Acadian teachers, lawyers, and politicians. These new leaders worked through the government to improve the lives of Acadians.

World War II (1939–1945) brought better economic times to both Acadians and English-speakers. Workers started mining the province's coal, which was used to make steel for weapons. At the port of Saint John, dockworkers loaded ships with war supplies bound for the battlefields of Europe. And the province's shipyards bustled to repair damaged battleships.

When the war was over, New Brunswick's economy slumped once again. New Brunswickers struggled until the 1960s, when the government offered loans to new businesses, many of which wanted to make use of the

Canadian troops stationed in Saint John during World War II parade through the city.

province's natural resources. Farming, lumbering, fishing, and mining boomed again. The government also helped more residents pay for their schooling and for job training.

Although the province's economy was improving, the gap between Acadians and English-speakers was slower to close. To help make these groups feel like equal communities within the province, the New Brunswick government passed a law in 1969 that made both English and French the province's official languages. And in 1993, an amendment, or change, to the Canadian constitution gave New Brunswick's English-speaking and French-speaking communities equal status in the province. This means that each group has a legal right to preserve its culture through its own schools and organizations. Although Acadians and English-speakers still disagree on some issues, together they are working hard to improve life in their province.

Loggers, Miners, Fishers, and Farmers

Thick forests, valuable minerals, fish-filled waters, and fertile soil. New Brunswickers count on these natural resources and the products made from them to provide jobs and keep the province's economy strong.

With trees covering 90 percent of New Brunswick, forests are the province's most important natural resource. Although only 1 percent of the workforce has jobs in forestry, many other laborers sell or make wood products from trees. In fact, about one-fourth of all goods made in New Brunswick are related to forestry.

Most of New Brunswick's trees are ground into wood pulp, which is made into newsprint, boxes, bags, and other paper goods. Every year, loggers cut down about one million Christmas trees, most of which are shipped to the United States. Other forest products include maple syrup, lumber, and furniture.

Loggers use big machines, such as skidders (below), *as well as small chain saws* (right) *to harvest trees from New Brunswick's forests.*

TIMBER!

Clarence's career in New Brunswick's forests began when he was a teenager in the 1950s. At first he helped his father and grandfather cut firewood for their family. When he was 18, he and a friend began cutting and selling wood for a living. They paid a woodlot owner for the trees on the lot and harvested them. One man cut down the timber with an ax, while his partner yarded, or took the trees out to the road and stacked them. To help haul the timber across rough terrain, the men used a yarding horse.

Clarence still works in forestry, but the equipment he uses now is very different. These days loggers cut down trees with power saws and yard with large tractors called skidders. Some forest workers harvest trees with even more complex machines. A feller buncher, for example, can reach out a mechanical arm to chop down a tree, limb it (remove its branches), cut it to a certain length, and stack the logs on the ground. Because of these advanced machines, Clarence's job is easier, and New Brunswick's forestry industry is booming.

New Brunswick's forests are exposed to many dangers. Fires and **acid precipitation**—a mixture of rain or snow and air pollution—have destroyed some of the province's woodlands. Budworms harm spruce and fir trees by chewing through the needles. In addition, some logging companies cut down more trees than they replant. Foresters are studying ways to help New Brunswick's forests thrive. These experts work to preserve wilderness areas for future loggers, as well as for vacationers who like to hunt, fish, and hike in the forests.

Mining wasn't a big business in New Brunswick until the mid-1900s, when metals were discovered near Bathurst and Miramichi in the northern part of the province. Workers then started mining silver, lead, and zinc.

Deep underground, workers mine stibnite—a mineral that contains antimony. Antimony is used to make medicines, paint, and matches.

Nowadays New Brunswick mines more zinc than any other province in Canada. And the province is the nation's second largest producer of lead and silver.

A livestock farmer mows hay to feed his animals.

Coal mined at Minto near Grand Lake fuels two electric power plants. Potash scooped up in Sussex is made into fertilizer. In the northeast, workers harvest peat moss, which is mixed into potting soil. Other deposits mined in the province include copper, antimony, bismuth, and gold. Although only 1 percent of New Brunswick's workers are miners, they help the province earn a lot of money.

About 2 percent of workers in New Brunswick farm for a living. Farmers plant potatoes—the province's most important crop—in the rich soil of the Saint John River valley. Some of the potatoes are seed potatoes, from which more potatoes are grown. Most of the province's seed potatoes are shipped to farmers in the United States. Table potatoes are sold fresh in markets or are processed into french fries. Fruits grown in New Brunswick include apples, strawberries, and blueberries.

Livestock owners harvest hay and oats to feed dairy cows, beef cattle, hogs, and chickens. Dairy cows in New Brunswick produce all the milk the province

New Brunswick's fishers use fish traps called weirs (left) **to catch sardines. On shore, fishers unload their catch** (right), **which is sent to markets or food-processing plants.**

needs. Workers process some of the milk into cheese and butter.

About 2 percent of working New Brunswickers have jobs in the fishery (fishing industry). In the Northumberland Strait and the Bay of Fundy, fishers bring in lobsters and snow crabs—the province's most valuable catches. Overfishing has reduced the number of lobsters in recent years. So the government limits the lobster season to make sure that lobsters in Canadian waters don't die out.

In the Bay of Fundy, fishers set up weirs. These horseshoe-shaped net fences are used to trap sardines, or young herring. Fishers also haul in bluefin tuna, which is sold mainly to Japan.

Some fishers in New Brunswick are developing a new industry called **aquaculture**—the growing of fish in tanks or in floating cages or nets. These fish farmers raise Atlantic salmon, rainbow trout, mussels, and oysters for sale to grocery stores and restaurants. Aquaculture has become a big business in New Brunswick as the number of fish in the province's ocean waters decrease.

Much of the fish harvested in New Brunswick is brought to the province's food-processing plants. At these factories, workers smoke salmon, freeze snow crabs and lobsters, and pack tuna and sardines into cans. Some companies make soft drinks and baked goods. Food processing is one of the largest manufacturing industries in New Brunswick.

Other manufacturers in the province rely on different natural resources. From trees and mineral products, paper, chemicals, and metal goods are made. In shipyards, builders craft steel

Workers in paper mills (facing page) *turn New Brunswick's trees into cardboard boxes, paper bags, and newsprint. Some service workers sell fruits, vegetables, cheeses, and baked goods at the City Market* (right) *in Saint John.*

military vessels. About 12 percent of New Brunswick's workers earn a living from manufacturing.

Most New Brunswickers—76 percent—hold jobs in the service industry. Service workers help other people and businesses. Politicians, teachers, plumbers, and store clerks all have service jobs. Many service workers in New Brunswick have transportation jobs in Saint John, a shipping center, and Moncton—a hub for the trucking industry. The telecommunications industry also employs many residents.

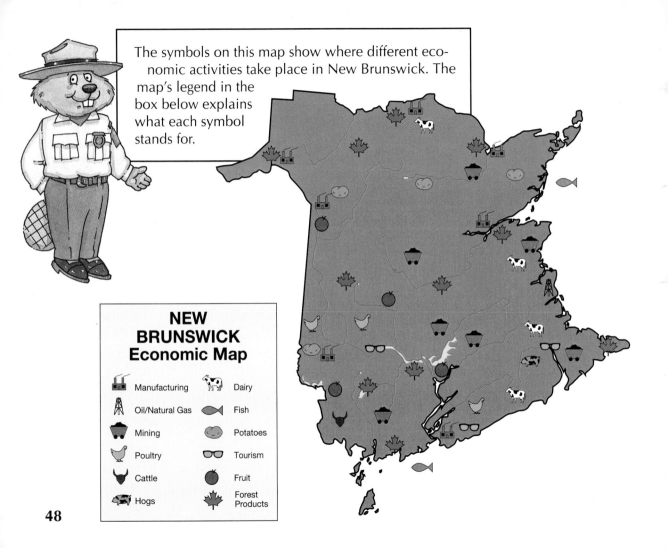

The symbols on this map show where different economic activities take place in New Brunswick. The map's legend in the box below explains what each symbol stands for.

NEW BRUNSWICK Economic Map

- Manufacturing
- Oil/Natural Gas
- Mining
- Poultry
- Cattle
- Hogs
- Dairy
- Fish
- Potatoes
- Tourism
- Fruit
- Forest Products

Rafters tie inner tubes together for a wild ride down the Saint Croix River. Tourists flock to New Brunswick to enjoy the province's many rivers.

One of the most important service industries in the province is tourism. Workers in this industry serve food in restaurants, run hotels, and guide tours. New Brunswick's rugged forests, amazing tides, and warm beaches bring visitors in droves. People camp, hike, and canoe in Fundy National Park and Kouchibouguac National Park. With so much to see and do in New Brunswick's great outdoors, it's no wonder that tourists flock to the Picture Province.

A Community of Cultures

If you drew a diagonal line across New Brunswick from the northwest to the southeast, you'd divide the province into two triangles. New Brunswick's French-speaking community lives mainly in the northeastern triangle. Most English-speakers make their homes in the southwestern triangle.

English and French— New Brunswick's two official languages— appear on signs throughout the province.

New Brunswick's two main groups are proud to be known as two unique communities. New Brunswick is Canada's only officially **bilingual** province. This means that the provincial government offers all services in French and in English. In courts, for example, many lawyers and judges speak both languages. And schools offer classes in French and English.

Of the 724,000 people in New Brunswick, about 32 percent are Acadians. They are descendants of the first Acadians who came to New Brunswick from France in the 1600s. Nowadays more Acadians live in New Brunswick than anywhere else in the world.

Fishing, farming, and lumbering have long been a part of the Acadian way of life. In recent years, some Acadians have found work in the mines of the northeast. Moncton is known as the unofficial capital of the Acadian region. Here Acadians work in French-language libraries and museums and attend classes in French at the Université de Moncton.

Acadians throughout the province work to preserve their heritage. The Acadian Historical Village in Cara-quet shows what life was like for Acadians in the 1800s. Visitors to the village can try spinning wool into yarn, grinding grain into flour, or printing a newspaper. At the yearly Acadian Festival in Caraquet, Acadians share their food, art, and crafts. Music is a big part of Acadian culture, and Acadian choirs have won many awards.

At the Acadian Historical Village in Caraquet, Acadians dress as their ancestors did in the 1800s.

A blacksmith explains his craft to a visitor (top) *and a choir* (bottom) *performs at King's Landing, a Loyalist historical site.*

English-speakers make up about 62 percent of New Brunswick's population. Many are the descendants of English Loyalists, who arrived from the eastern United States in the late 1700s. Others have ancestors who came from Ireland and Scotland during the 1800s to work in the shipyards and other industries. English-speakers live mainly in and around Saint John, Fredericton, and other cities in the southern and western parts of the province.

The Loyalist heritage is preserved at Kings Landing Historical Settlement near Fredericton. Guides lead tours through houses and other buildings that date from the 1800s. During the summer, children can live on the settlement for a week. They go to a one-room school and help with chores, such as making soap or carrying water.

At the Irish Festival in Miramichi, a drummer beats in time to traditional Irish music.

A large Irish community lives in Miramichi, an English-speaking city in the heart of the Acadian region. The Irish Festival—Canada's oldest and largest Irish celebration—is held here every year. Fiddlers play lively tunes as dancers step to the music. And visitors have fun playing Irish games and sampling traditional dishes.

Native peoples make up about 1 percent of New Brunswick's population. Some Micmacs and Maliseets make their homes in the province's cities, but most live in the northeast on **reserves**—lands set aside for Native peoples. Many continue to speak their traditional languages and work to keep their customs alive.

55

For many years, Native people were denied opportunities available to white people. As a result, some Native people have had trouble finding jobs and have less money than most New Brunswickers. But as more education and training are offered to Native people, their standard of living is improving. On some reserves, Native people have opened new businesses to help their communities earn more money.

Immigrants from the Caribbean, South America, Africa, Asia, and eastern Europe also call New Brunswick home. Most of these groups have settled in Saint John, Fredericton, and Moncton. Caribbean Days and the Chinese August Moon Festival are just two of the many celebrations these newcomers have brought to New Brunswick.

Native Roots

Micmacs from the Eel River Bar Reserve in northern New Brunswick are creating a garden full of plants that their ancestors once used for medicine and food. The Aboriginal Heritage Garden, which will cover 110 acres (44.5 hectares) of land in Chaleur Beach Provincial Park, will look like the New Brunswick landscape did before Europeans settled the region.

Through this project, Native people have learned about their culture. They want to share this knowledge with the garden's visitors. As a tourist attraction, the Aboriginal Heritage Garden will also bring jobs and money to the Eel River Bar Reserve. This income will help the Micmac community thrive.

New Brunswickers of all backgrounds flock to popular music festivals. At the Miramichi Folk Song Festival, performers play traditional Maritime songs. Jazz lovers enjoy the Harvest Jazz and Blues Festival in Fredericton. Saint John's Festival by the Sea attracts musicians from across the country.

Some other festivals in New Brunswick celebrate food. People enjoy seafood at the Salmon Festival in Campbellton and at the Lobster Festival in Shediac. At the Chocolate Festival in Saint Stephen, kids compete to see who can eat the most chocolate pudding! In early spring, New Brunswickers collect sap from maple trees to make maple sugar and candy at sugaring-off celebrations.

New Brunswickers and tourists alike enjoy many outdoor activities, including skiing (facing page left), sailboarding (facing page right), and hiking (right).

No matter what the season, New Brunswickers find plenty to do outdoors. In spring and summer, canoers and white-water rafters head to the province's swift rivers. Windsurfers and sailors ride the ocean waves. Hikers enjoy the quiet of the province's thick forests. Golf, soccer, and baseball are also popular sports, and fishers snag trout at busy fishing holes.

In winter New Brunswickers lace on their skates for rousing games of ice hockey. Ice-fishers drill holes in the frozen rivers and lakes. Downhill skiers hit the steep slopes, while cross-country skiers glide across the frozen landscape.

New Brunswick is a land of variety, with natural beauty, valuable resources, and a rich history. Above all, the people—including Acadians, British, Irish, Micmacs, and Maliseets—have given New Brunswick an identity all its own.

Famous New Brunswickers

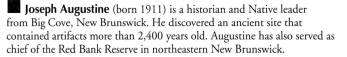

1 William Maxwell Aitken (Lord Beaverbrook) (1879–1964), from Newcastle, New Brunswick, moved to London, England in 1910. There he was elected to Parliament and became a baron in 1917. He took the name Beaverbrook after a stream near his home in Canada. After leaving politics, Beaverbrook started a chain of successful British newspapers.

Joseph Augustine (born 1911) is a historian and Native leader from Big Cove, New Brunswick. He discovered an ancient site that contained artifacts more than 2,400 years old. Augustine has also served as chief of the Red Bank Reserve in northeastern New Brunswick.

3 Richard Bedford Bennett (1870–1947)—a businessman, lawyer, and politician—was born in Hopewell, New Brunswick. Bennett led Canada's Conservative Party from 1927 to 1938, serving as the country's prime minister from 1930 to 1935.

Miller Brittain (1912–1968) was an artist whose early paintings depict the daily lives of people in New Brunswick. His later works include religious subjects and pastel landscapes. Brittain lived in Saint John.

5 Edith Butler (born 1942), a singer and songwriter from Paquetville, New Brunswick, has popularized Acadian culture through her music. She has performed Acadian folksongs around the world and has earned many honors, including the Order of Canada.

60

6 **Bliss Carman** (1861–1929), born in Fredericton, worked as an editor, writer, and lecturer. Also a poet, Carman was known for his verses about the Canadian landscape. His poetry volumes include *Low Tide on Grand Pré, The Pipes of Pan,* and *Sappho.*

■ **Herménégilde Chiasson** (born 1946) is an Acadian filmmaker, playwright, poet, and sculptor. Through his work, Chiasson has tried to change the stereotypical view of Acadians by showing their rich and varied culture. Chiasson was born in Saint-Simon, New Brunswick.

8 **Julia Catherine (Beckwith) Hart** (1796–1867) was born in Fredericton. Her novel *St. Ursula's Convent,* which she wrote at age 17, was the first work of fiction by a native-born Canadian to be published in Canada. Hart's book reflects both her English and French backgrounds.

9 **Kenneth Colin Irving** (1899–1992), from Bouctouche, New Brunswick, built a successful business empire from a small chain of automobile service stations. Known as one of Canada's leading industrialists, Irving owned more than 300 companies in industries such as oil, lumber, shipping, and food processing.

■ **Antonine Maillet** (born 1929) is a novelist from Bouctouche. Her books—including *La Sagouine* and *Pélagie-la-Charrette*—describe the land, history, and people of Acadia. Many of Maillet's works have been turned into plays.

11 **Harrison McCain** (born 1927, *left*) and his brother **Wallace McCain** (born 1930) built eastern Canada's first frozen french-fry plant in 1957. This business became an international food-processing empire, producing foods ranging from fruit juice to pizza. The McCain brothers live in Florenceville, New Brunswick.

12 **Frank McKenna** (born 1948), from Apohaqui, New Brunswick, is a lawyer and politician. He has been the leader of the Liberal Party of New Brunswick since 1985 and has served two terms as the province's premier.

13 **Don Messer** (1909–1973) was born in Tweedside, New Brunswick. Through radio and television, he and his band, the Islanders, brought traditional fiddle and dance music into Canadian homes. Messer and the Islanders also recorded more than 30 albums.

■ **Graydon Nicholas** (born 1946) is a lawyer and judge from the Tobique Reserve in New Brunswick. Throughout his career, he has focused on Native issues and treaty rights. In 1991 Nicholas was appointed to the Provincial Court, becoming the first Native judge in the Maritime provinces.

15 **Peter Paul** (1902–1989) was an expert on Maliseet language and culture and on Native issues. A member of the Order of Canada, Paul was also awarded an honorary doctorate degree by the University of New Brunswick for his contributions to Native studies. Paul was born in Woodstock, New Brunswick.

16 **David Adams Richards** (born 1950), from Newcastle, New Brunswick, writes about the people of the Miramichi region in northeastern New Brunswick. His books include *The Coming of Winter* and *Nights Below Station Street*—a novel that earned Richards the Governor General's Award.

17 **Charles G. D. Roberts** (1860–1943) was a teacher and writer from Fredericton. Considered the Father of Canadian Literature, Roberts is known for his books about animals and nature. His works include *Eyes of the Wilderness* and *Earth's Enigmas*.

18 **Brenda Mary Robertson** (born 1929) lives in Shediac, New Brunswick. In 1967 she became the first woman elected to the New Brunswick legislature. Robertson was reelected four times and was appointed to the Senate of Canada in 1984.

19 **Donald Sutherland** (born 1934) is an actor known for playing a wide range of characters. He has appeared in more than 65 films, including *The Dirty Dozen, M*A*S*H,* and *Ordinary People.* Sutherland was born in Saint John.

20 **Samuel Leonard Tilley** (1818–1896) was a politician from Gagetown, New Brunswick. Elected to four terms in the New Brunswick Assembly, Tilley later served as the province's lieutenant-governor. During his time in office, Tilley helped New Brunswick enter Confederation.

21 **Roch Voisine** (born 1961) is a singer and songwriter who performs in both English and French. His recordings are especially popular in French-speaking regions of Canada and in France, where his first album, *Hélène,* sold more than one million copies. Voisine was born in Saint-Basile, New Brunswick.

22 **John Clarence Webster** (1863–1950), from Shediac, was a surgeon who wrote about medicine and other scientific subjects. As a retired doctor, Webster turned to historical research and helped start up museums in Saint John and Fort Beauséjour.

Fast Facts

Provincial Symbols

Motto: *Spem reduxit* (Hope was restored)
Nickname: Picture Province, Loyalist Province
Tree: balsam fir
Bird: black-capped chickadee
Flower: purple violet
Tartan: forest green for lumbering, meadow green for
agriculture, blue for coastal and inland waters, gold for
the province's potential wealth, and red for the loyalty
and devotion of the early Loyalist settlers and the Royal
New Brunswick Regiment

Provincial Highlights

Landmarks: Covered Bridge in Hartland, Flowerpot
Rocks at Hopewell Cape, Magnetic Hill in Moncton,
Reversing Falls in Saint John, Fundy National Park near
Alma, Roosevelt Campobello International Park on
Campobello Island, Kouchibouguac National Park near
Kouchibouguac, Grand Falls in Grand Falls, Kings
Landing Historical Settlement, New Brunswick Museum
in Saint John

Annual events: Salmon Festival in Campbellton (June),
Festival International de la Francophonie in Tracadie-
Sheila (July), Lobster Festival in Shediac (July), Loyalist
City Festival in Saint John (July), Festival by the Sea in
Saint John (Aug.), Miramichi Folk Song Festival (Aug.),
Festival Acadien in Caraquet (Aug.), Atlantic Balloon
Festival in Sussex (Sept.), Harvest Jazz and Blues Festival
in Fredericton (Sept.)

Population

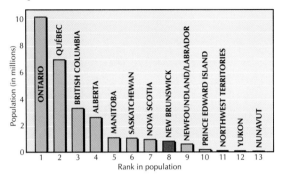

Population*: 724,000
Rank in population, nationwide: 8th
Population distribution: 48 percent urban; 52 percent
rural
Population density: 26.2 people per sq mi (10.1 per
sq km)
Capital: Fredericton (46,466)
Major cities and towns (and populations*): Saint
John (74,969), Moncton (57,010), Riverview (16,270),
Edmundston (10,835), Dieppe (10,463), Oromocto
(9,325), Campbellton (8,699)
Major ethnic groups*: British and French, 33 percent
each; multiple backgrounds, 31 percent; German and
Native peoples, 1 percent each; Dutch, Italian, Polish,
Scandinavian, Ukrainian, 1 percent total
*1991 census

Endangered Species

Mammals: eastern cougar
Birds: Harlequin duck, anatum peregrine falcon, piping plover
Plants: Furbish's lousewort

Geographic Highlights

Area (land/water): 28,355 sq mi (73,440 sq km)
Rank in area, nationwide: 11th
Highest point: Mount Carleton (2,680 ft/820 m)
Major rivers and lakes: Saint John River, Saint Croix River, Restigouche River, Miramichi River, Petitcodiac River, Grand Lake

Economy

Percentage of Workers Per Job Sector

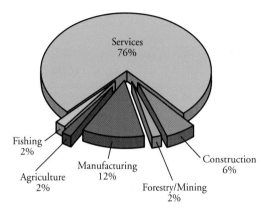

Services 76%
Fishing 2%
Agriculture 2%
Manufacturing 12%
Forestry/Mining 2%
Construction 6%

Natural resources: forests, copper, lead, silver, zinc, potash, coal, gold, peat, antimony, bismuth
Agricultural products: dairy cattle, potatoes, beef cattle, hogs, poultry, barley, hay, oats, blueberries, apples, strawberries, carrots, cauliflower, sweet corn
Manufactured goods: paper products, frozen French fries, baked goods, beer, dairy products, fish products, packaged meats, soft drinks, wood products, ships, fabricated metal products, chemicals

Energy

Electric power: petroleum or coal (35 percent), nuclear power (30 percent), hydroelectric (15 percent), imported power from utilities in other provinces (20 percent)

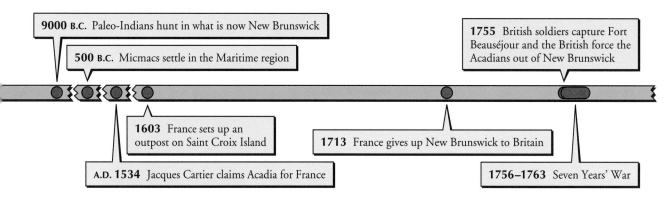

9000 B.C. Paleo-Indians hunt in what is now New Brunswick

500 B.C. Micmacs settle in the Maritime region

1755 British soldiers capture Fort Beauséjour and the British force the Acadians out of New Brunswick

1603 France sets up an outpost on Saint Croix Island

1713 France gives up New Brunswick to Britain

A.D. 1534 Jacques Cartier claims Acadia for France

1756–1763 Seven Years' War

Federal Government

Capital: Ottawa
Head of state: British Crown, represented by the governor general
Head of government: prime minister
Cabinet: ministers appointed by the prime minister
Parliament: Senate—104 members appointed by the governor general; House of Commons—295 members elected by the people
New Brunswick representation in parliament: 10 senators; 10 house members
Voting age: 18

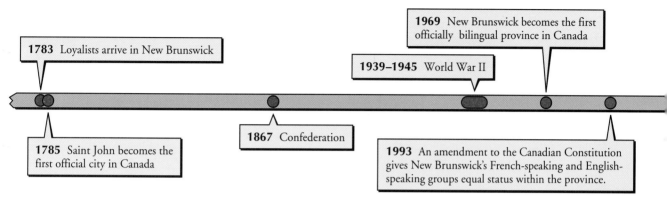

1783 Loyalists arrive in New Brunswick

1785 Saint John becomes the first official city in Canada

1867 Confederation

1939–1945 World War II

1969 New Brunswick becomes the first officially bilingual province in Canada

1993 An amendment to the Canadian Constitution gives New Brunswick's French-speaking and English-speaking groups equal status within the province.

Provincial Government

Capital: Fredericton
Crown Representative: lieutenant-governor
Head of government: premier
Cabinet: ministers appointed by the premier
Legislative Assembly: 58 members elected to terms that can last up to five years
Voting age: 18 years
Major political parties: Progressive Conservative, Liberal

Government Services

To help pay the people who work for New Brunswick's government, the people of New Brunswick pay taxes on money they earn and on many of the items they buy. The services run by the provincial government help assure the people of New Brunswick of a high quality of life. Government funds pay for medical care, for education, for road building and repairs, and for other facilities such as libraries and parks. In addition, the government has funds to help people who are disabled, elderly, or poor.

Glossary

acid precipitation   Rain or snow that contains chemical pollutants from the air. When combined with water, these pollutants form acids that can harm plants and animals.

aquaculture   The controlled raising of animals and plants in water to provide food for people.

bilingual   The use of two languages.

colony   A territory ruled by a country some distance away.

Confederation   The union of four British colonies under the British North America Act in 1867. Confederation formed the Dominion of Canada and set up two levels of government—national and provincial. Other provinces later joined the original four.

dike   A wall or dam built to keep a sea or river from overflowing.

immigrant   A person who moves into a foreign country and settles there.

Loyalist   A person who supports the government during a revolt.

peat bog   Wet, spongy ground that is rich in decaying plant matter (peat), which is sometimes dried for use as fuel.

reserve   Public land set aside by the government to be used by Native peoples.

wigwam   A kind of tent used by some Native peoples, shaped in a dome or cone and covered with bark, grasswoven mats, leaves, or other material.

Pronunciation Guide

Acadia (uh-KAY-dee-uh)

Appalachian (ap-uh-LAY-chuhn)

Beauséjour (boh-say-ZHOOR)

Cartier, Jacques (kahr-TYAY, ZHAHK)

Chaleur (shuh-LUHR)

Grand Manan (GRAND muh-NAN)

Kouchibouguac
(koo-shee-boo-GWAHK)

Miramichi (MIHR-uh-muh-SHEE)

Moncton (MUHNK-tuhn)

Nepisiguit (nuh-PIHZ-uh-gwuht)

Petitcodiac (peht-ee-KOHD-ee-ak)

Saint Croix (SAYNT KROY)

Index

About the Author

A freelance writer and editor, Kumari Campbell also owns her own marketing and public relations business. Originally from Sri Lanka, she moved to Canada when she was a teenager. Campbell lives with her husband and three children in Souris, Prince Edward Island.

Acknowledgments

Mapping Specialists Ltd., pp. 1, 12–13, 48; Benoît Chalifour, pp. 2, 42; Robert E. Cramer/Geographical Slides, p. 6; Artwork by Terry Boles, pp. 7, 12, 48, 65; Eugene Schulz, p. 7; © James P. Rowan, pp. 8, 16; Tourism New Brunswick, pp. 9, 10, 11, 22 (left), 22–23, 45 (right), 49, 50 (right), 53, 55, 58 (both), 59, 70; Voscar, The Maine Photographer, pp. 14, 15, 20 (both), 44, 45 (left), 46, 47, 52, 54 (both), 57, 69; David Dvorak, Jr., pp. 14 (inset), 18 (bottom); Jerry Hennen, p.17 (both); Cindy Kilgore Brown, pp. 18 (top), 19; Canadian Tourism Commission, p. 21; Artwork by Lewis Parker, collection University of Cape Breton, photograph by Michael Reppa, p. 25; National Archives of Canada, pp. 26 (C8028), 31 (C24550), 60 (top right—PA6467), 60 (left—C7733), 63 (middle left—PA12632); Laura Westlund, p. 27; Claude Picard, Artist/Commissioned by Canadian Heritage (Parks Canada), Atlantic Region, p. 29; Lewis Parker, Artist/Commissioned by Canadian Heritage (Parks Canada), Atlantic Region, p. 30; Confederation Life Gallery of Canadian History, p. 33; Provincial Archives of New Brunswick, pp. 34, 36–37, 39, 61 (top right), 61 (middle right), 62 (bottom), 63 (middle right); Eric Bagnell/New Brunswick Department of Natural Resources and Energy, pp. 41 (both), 43; City of Moncton, pp. 50 (left), 51; Yves Nantel, p. 60 (bottom right); University of New Brunswick Archives, p. 61 (middle left), 62 (middle left), 62 (middle right); Anthony Buckley and Constantine Limited, p. 61 (bottom left); McCain Foods Limited, p. 61 (bottom right); Communications New Brunswick, p. 62 (top left); Canadian Broadcasting Corporation, p. 62 (top right); Portrait of Senator Robertson by Michael Bedford Photography, p. 63 (top left); Hollywood Book and Poster, p. 63 (top right); CR Productions: Montreal, Canada, p. 63 (bottom).